The Earth Understands Me
POEMS TO HEAL A WILD HEART

Logan Hailey

Copyright © 2024 by Logan Hailey
Yarrow Books
an imprint of Yarrow Publishing
Logan Hailey Creative LLC
www.naturallylogan.com

All rights reserved.
No portion of this book may be reproduced
in any form or by any means
without written permission
from the publisher or author,
except as permitted by U.S. copyright law.

ISBN 979-8-9911497-1-6
U.S. Library of Congress Control Number
LCCN 2024917627

Printed in the United States of America

We are all of the Earth,
our souls inextricably intertwined
with the unbreakable golden threads of life.

Contents

Prelude	6
Dedication	8
Simple Delight	12
Loam	14
Sapling	18
Gratitude & Rapture	20
The Stray	22
First Law of Thermodynamics	24
Transformation	27
Reliability	28
Alchemical Foray	31
Mycorrhizal Love	33
How Dare You?	36
The Taker	38
The Giver	41
Why We Must Heal	42
Just Another	44
Do You See Me?	45
Springtime of Your Life	46
Greatness	48
Whims of Pastel Dawn	50
Where the Desert Ends	57
Aid for the Anxious Sailor	58
The Fisherman	64
A Wild Cloak	66
When I Die	68
Productivity	70
Expansion	72
You Say You're An Adventurer	75

Contents

I Am the Type to Weep Softly	76
Love Me Like the Moon	80
Footpaths	82
Should I Trust?	84
How We Change the World	86
Hulls	88
Spice	90
What is Meant for You	92
Because of the Mud	94
Nothing is Forever	96
I Like My Feet Dirty	98
Sensual Intricacy	100
Saturate Me	102
You're Blooming!	105
Currents of Eternity	106
Beautiful	109
Emptiness	110
The Sweetest Embrace	112
Solace	114
Choose the Marvelous	116
Spontaneous Whims	118
Now Everything Makes Sense	120
The Grizzly Queen	122
Trees Need Mulch	124
They Tried	127
Defiance!	128
Can We Talk About the Good?	130
Nature's Reminders	133
Paradise is a State of Mind	136

Prelude

From the moment we are born into the industrialized world, we are taught that our belonging is conditional: a matter of our attractiveness, outward success, intelligence, or the contributions we can make to the societal machine. We are bombarded with confusion and lies to make us forget that we are native creatures of the Earth with intrinsic value, just like the willows and warblers, moose and morels, octopus and oaks.

Instead, we are taught that the Earth is *out there*, completely isolated from humans who reside inside the confines of buildings and synthetic cities. This indoctrination incites a painful separateness—the illusion of humankind versus nature, or the individual versus the collective. Within this artificial paradigm, we no longer belong and live *with* the land, but merely extract *from* it, as if all the intricacies of the natural world are merely inanimate resources for exploitation and use. It is no surprise that this mindset bridges over into people's treatment of eachother, too.

Society seeks to exploit this delusion, as if dominating nature into submission will somehow exalt our species above the rest. But nobody wins in a war against oneself. In reality, we are all part of the same intricate web, each person and wild creature with their own unique gifts and offerings to the ecosystem as a whole.

We do not have to live in isolation from the Earth, yet modernity has divorced us from the very essence of our humanness, chiseling away our connections to Self, Community, and Purpose. This separateness provokes a deep hunger of the soul. It is a hunger that the vacuous pit of consumerism and numbness can never fill.

If your journey has been anything like mine, perhaps you have tried to satiate your rumbling belly with futile searches for wholeness and belonging—wearing costumes or performing for hollow accolades, chasing superficial markers of success, morphing yourself to be more likable by others, trying to change for a romantic partner, numbing yourself with alcohol or intoxicants, isolating yourself, avoiding difficult emotions, hiding your creative longings, or otherwise betraying your true nature for the sake of acceptance.

These forms of pseudo-belonging are similar to a junk food meal; temporarily satisfying, yet harmful to our vitality, leaving us deficient in the essential vitamins of connection and self-love.

When we remember how long our species has lived under open skies, the consequences of the recent shift to synthetic living are woefully unsurprising. Of course, estrangement from the Earth yields an unexplainable yearning within! Our culture's dis-ease, apathy, mental illness, relational decay, and overwhelming grief are natural responses to unnatural ways of living. Many of us are starving for something deeper, something more, something *real*.

Nature is trying to call us back home to a space where we are always understood and welcome. When we reunite with the land and sea in a respectful and loving way, we also reconnect with ourselves and the vital life force of what it means to be alive on this planet. The wild soul of things has been forgotten and suppressed under the weight of artificiality, but its light cannot be dimmed, and neither can yours.

So, how do we restore? Though the outer world often seems overwhelmingly sick, the solutions to our ailments can be simple and free. Healing your own wild heart and reigniting your personal authenticity is a gift to the ecosystem at large. Change always begins with the Self.

We can return our feet to the soil and our skin to the sun. Lean into our discomfort rather than away from it. Feel fully rather than numbing and avoiding. Sit with the plants and the wild creatures, giving them attention, adoration, and respect. Though they speak a quiet, subtle language far different than ours, we can listen to them in the ways we long to be listened to, and engage in the same reciprocity with other people, too.

Most importantly, we can slow down and embrace silence amidst a world of chaotic noise and distractions. Try to follow the poetic seasonal rhythms of the land. Grow and forage sustenance for our bodies. Seek productive nourishment for our minds. Learn, taste, and explore the realms beyond fear. Remember that you belong here.

I hope these poems inspire you to dig deeper in your exploration of emotional landscapes. Just like the diverse ecosystems that surround us, every internal experience has something to offer. If we sit with the wild parts of ourselves and integrate them into the whole, we can be free again.

This book is dedicated to anyone
who has ever felt lost
or heartbroken
or outcasted
or ashamed
or unworthy
or unaccepted
for who you are.

You are an integral strand
in the web of life.

Every cell inside of you contains
the same things
as flowers, forests,
butterflies, birds, bees,
and whales swimming in infinite seas.

Any time you feel lost,
remember to just go outside.

Nature is always calling you home.

She will hold you.
She will help you regrow.
She will tear away the costumes
and reveal the truth
which is wild, untainted peace
inside of you.

The Earth understands you,
so you can never be alone.

Simple Delight

There is simple delight in the melody
of chickadees in the morning

delicate droplets dripping from the oak
who stood last night—a bold wise man—
alone in the storm, unshaken.

There is simple delight
in the way I inhale his exhales,

oxygen moved through a million lungs
only momentarily in my chest. Tell me,
have you breathed it, too?

There is simple delight
in knowing that the Earth understands me
nothing needs be explained.

She accepts me for all my glory,
my flaws, mistakes, my pain.

We dance together no matter the weather,
she dabs my tears with rain.

I do not need grand gestures;
designers and jewels do not excite.

I am satisfied by the simplest of things.
I want the Earth's delights.

an open heart is loamy soil,
rich and fertile
for a new earth
growing love eternal
coaxing pain into rebirth

a closed heart is
sheathed in stone
seemingly safe
but forever alone

(nothing good can grow
in suffocation below
yearning left unspoken)

even when it hurts,
my dear, please stay soft
do not let them pave you
do not them spray you
with poison

do not let them convince you
that concrete
is better than loam

(a closed heart is a place
where only darkness
grows)

When you fall in love with nature,
you fall in love with yourself.

Sapling

I asked the trees,
What's happening to me?
It feels like I am dying.

Gingko advised,
"Drop old leaves."
Maple apprised,
"Release your seeds."
Redwood whispered,
"Soon you'll be free."

My trunk collapsed
yet my roots remained.
My heartwood cracked;
all I felt was pain.

Please can a fire
burn it all away?
I don't want to be me
anymore,
I'd pray.

Pine replied,
"Patience, child."
Spruce smiled,
"Remain wild."
Hemlock promised,
"Just breathe awhile."

Dormant frigid grey,
My old life decayed.
I stood naked, barren,
nothing left to say.

Until, at last, spring came,
sprouts burst
from my base.
The whole forest sang,
"We knew you'd be okay!"

Clouds brought me water,
fungi brought me food,
and the wise old trees
enriched my roots.

I grew
& grew.

Centuries passed.
Sturdy & strong,
my crown towering at last.

One autumn day
I looked down in the shade
to a young sapling
struggling & afraid.

What's happening to me?
she asked,
It feels like I am dying.

"No my love,"
I bowed my branch,
"You are just reviving."

Gratitude & Rapture

                Keep far away from me
those with their mouth full of knowing
        their mind full of boasting
           as if they can explain
            the magic or mystery
             of universal domain

Keep close to me
those with their nose pressed to flowers
their eyes wrinkled with laughter
as if they cannot contain
their gratitude and rapture
for life's wild terrain

When I was young
I was separate
desperate to belong

a lone stray always
on the outside
looking in
betrayed by the hope
I could ever fit in

(Can I please be a part
of something?)
I always felt apart
my groomed mask
could not outsmart

they all knew
I was a fraud)
like a stray dog
pretending
to have a home

(What does it feel like
to belong?)
for their approval
I longed

but the poodles scoffed
at my paws—too muddied
the greyhounds mocked
my cheeks—too pudgy

the retrievers gawked
at my fur—too scruffy
the street dogs laughed
at my mind well-studied

too much
or too little
for everyone
it seemed

The Stray

I untucked my tail
off validation
I weaned
I perked up my ears
licked my wounds clean
tore off my collar
nothing could tame me

I felt better separate
no longer
desperate
to be
part of some pack
plagued by conformity

alone a stray
always
on the outside—
I stopped
looking in

I belonged only
to the wild and the wind
howling along
to my own song
I became my own best friend

First Law of Thermodynamics

The best moments of your life
are not behind you, but ahead.
What if everything you've lost
made room for what's next?

Trust that life removed them for a reason.
Trust the lessons to prepare your next season.
Energy cannot be created nor destroyed,
so any love you gave away *will* be overjoyed

to return to you in a different form,
ebullient, unexpected and new.
Nothing shared from a genuine place
can ever be taken from you.

No one knew
the darkness of your cocoon
yet all along you were

transforming

Reliability

Nature saves me
not just once, but daily
she pulls me, gently
out of my cluttered mind
back into the world where I
am merely another creature
like the birch or porcupine

no matter my tears
or dreary skies
she looks at me
with fireweed eyes
smiling
into my loneliest parts.

                    Nature saves me
               not just once, but daily
            she grounds me, reliably
           solid in her dirt, while
         shaky people are full
           of disappointments

               the Earth always
                follows through
(everywhere, something
                 is still growing,
             blossoming anew)
          Nature always does
                    exactly
what she promised to do.

Mushrooms make magic out of decay so of course I'll alchemize my pain into a glorious foray against everything that tried to rot me!

Mycorrhizal Love

hold my hand the way that trees do
intertwine your roots with mine
let the mycelium colonize
our every vein and bone

hold my hand the way that fungi
interweave everything alive
like the whole globe would fall apart
without the web they've sewn

How Dare You?

For thousands of years, your ancestors chose desirable mates for their attractive traits. They hunted & fished, foraged & wished for the best lives for their children. From all the way down the line, they live in you like a capsule of time: your skin & your hair, your nose & your eyes. When you mope in the mirror or wear a disguise, surely your ancestors sigh—we fought so hard to survive just so you could be alive *and how dare you think you are unworthy?*

Imagine spending your whole life
trying to fit in with dogs...

Only to realize you were a wolf all along.

The Taker

Your skin was night
I was the moon
Glowing in your deceitful cocoon

Your arms were roots
I was the dirt
You burrowed & dug into my earth

Your lips were wild fruit
I was a hungry fawn
Left parched & alone at dawn

Your touch was lightning
Through my sky misguided
Cloudless when our storm subsided

You were the taker
I was the giver
My raindrops lost in your roaring river

The Giver

Imagine a lover...
(You shudder—love,
for you, only ever yielded pain)

But imagine a lover
as sweet as Mother
Earth in all her giving.

Why We Must Heal

I've never associated wisdom with age
And my assertion was confirmed one day
With a girl about the age of five

Her puppy bit me as I tried
To pull a thorn from its tiny paw
Sharp teeth in skin led blood to draw

The little girl looked at me with alarm and dread
With an apology, she bowed her head,

"I'm sorry, he didn't mean to hurt you!
He only used his teeth
'cuz he was hurting, too."

Just Another

I love being a romantic, but sometimes I wish
I could just look at life and see it for *what it is.*

I see soulful secrets growing in the forest
but to you, it's *just* a group of trees.

I feel the sunset soak in my bones
but to you, it's *just* reds, blues, pinks.

When I looked at you, I saw poems written in the stars.
I saw magic enshrining your scars.
But then you turned cold. You put up the walls.

(Now I wonder if maybe
you were *just another* person after all.)

No — I'll always be a romantic!
Because it's never *just* a tree.
It's never *just* a sunset, not for me!

My reality really is *that* deep; drenched in profundity.
But over-romanticizing people seems to be my specialty.

I love being a romantic, but still I wish
I could've just seen you the way that you saw me:

as *just another* person,
another sunset,
another tree.

Do You See Me?

The forest is much like a person: dense & layered & **longing to be known**. Entire worlds, microcosms exist within the whole. But at first glance, most only see **thickets of green**. Some stop for a moment, a photo, to hear robins sing (but just one note), quickly they move, *always on their way*, in a rush to find something new. Perhaps this is the modern world's disease: We meet people, we go places, **we look but do not always see**. It takes more time to pause & fully percieve the intricacies, complexities; nature requires *patience & inquiry*. Will you take the time to **unravel the mysteries** at your feet? Will you have the courage to defy superficiality & **dive deep**? The forest is more than a blanket of green; there is so much inside each of us *yearning* to be **seen**.

It is the springtime of your life! & the ocotillos are blooming their defiant red torches. On a dry eastbound morning through the sand, you can make peace with leaving (because going is always coming) & you always end up where you're supposed to be. At every goodbye, cry shamelessly because returning is inevitable & it is a blessing to feel all the moods & hues of existence. What a bore to be bland. The horizon is ever-brightening. Your soul is ever-ripening.

Greatness

A simple life is not complacency
Trust me, I *do* want to be great
Not great like a skyscraper or a billionaire
but great like a mountain of granite
unmoved by millenia
of everyone trying
to weather
him.

Dawn breaks the darkness in a hazy glow of red & gold above deep distant blue (*I wonder who painted over infinity?*) The beach is quiet, boardwalk empty, brass street lanterns barely awake with me, shining sepia along the shore.

Have you ever thought about the way **old pains dissipate?** Like salt in seawater, they vanish, ionize, scab over. You don't even think of them anymore.

There are, of course, wounds that never fully mend, but time numbs them and with each cycle of the rising and setting sun, **more peace seeps into the emptiness**.

Look up. Sky brighter, waves calmer, glow growing, *dawn inching along silent and mysterious* behind the shadow cloud horizon.

A ship emerges far in the distance from the frothy milk fog resting on the horizon of the great Atlantic. Three little birds scamper along the part of wet sand that was illuminated last night by the full moon's beam of white as if it was the sky's flashlight.

Have you ever thought about the way nothing makes sense in the moment,

yet as hours, days & years pass, **the sun of hindsight — the Light of Wisdom** — rises over your previously limited perception and you realize *what you did not know before*:

the **teachings of tribulations lap onto the shores of time** and the past is illuminated by understanding.

It *had to happen that way* so you could learn & grow & re-emerge; so that the **whims of oceanic fate could regurgitate your fragile complex bones** *here* on *this* sandy beach.

Look up. Sky peachy pink and pale yellow. Silver birds with long legs strut along the shore with a confident knowing — *the knowing that they are intrinsically of this beach.*

They **belong amidst the sand & sea**, and they need not be bothered with these human things.

Human thoughts: What are thoughts anyways? Mere reflections on the *shimmering salt waves* of our big round heads?

Mirrors of our minds which reflect upwards the **intangible feelings of our hearts?** Random spatterings of seagull shit on the windshield of morning?

Indefinable uncontainable wisps of seabreeze wind that blow into our hair-covered skulls and out again

with the **whims of things we do not understand and probably never will,** but think about anyways because thoughts always beget more thoughts.

But the sea, the blue sea, the dream sea, the salt-filled, whale-swimming, wave-rushing sea: *She does not think of me!*

She is *far too busy* birthing pastel sunrises and fiery balls of light out of the **Womb of her endless horizon.**

*The sea never tells any lies
everything here is Real*

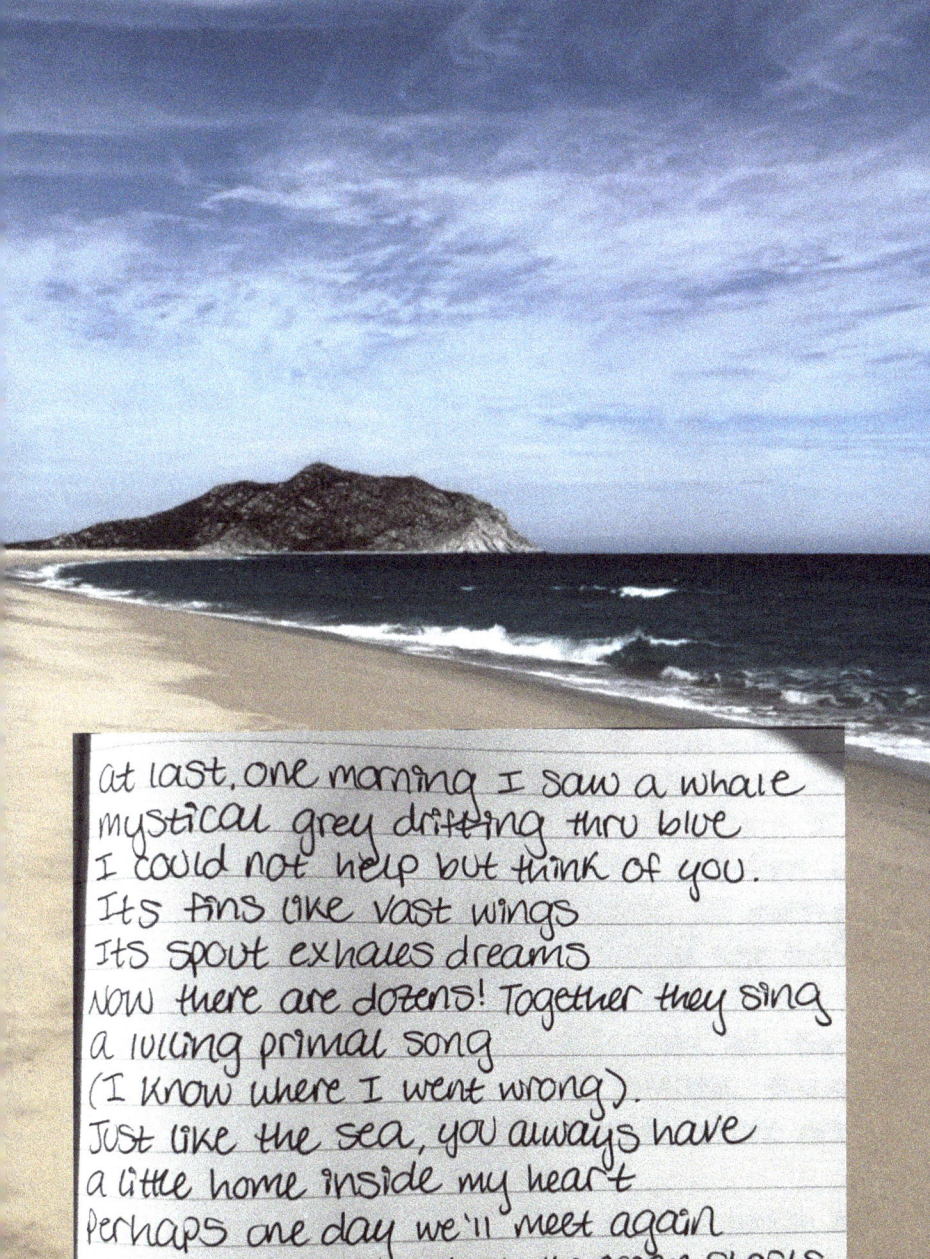

At last, one morning I saw a whale
mystical grey drifting thru blue
I could not help but think of you.
Its fins like vast wings
Its spout exhales dreams
Now there are dozens! Together they sing
a lulling primal song
(I know where I went wrong).
Just like the sea, you always have
a little home inside my heart
Perhaps one day we'll meet again
where the desert ends & the ocean starts.

Aid for the Anxious Sailor

Maybe you don't need
to have it all figured out.
Maybe you don't want to know
what happens next.

If you saw the mountain view
at the start of the trail,
would you still take the hike?
If you knew the bright ending
of some fairytale book,
would you still read the type?

If the adventure was
mapped in familiarity
would you still embark?
If you knew that love
ends in solemn aches
would you ignore the spark?

What a boring life
to hold outcomes in one's hand
white knuckle grip on the helm
steering straight toward the land
believing fate is in your command.

No! I want the wild ocean
the excitement of suspense,
the work & waves,
patience that staves
off gratification
the waits & delays

that tangible tension
between the sailor & the sea
a foaming oasis
of all the beauty
that can be
(maybe)

we're blind to what's next
(and that's for the best)
for the ocean is infinitely deep—
I don't care to see
the bottom, nor render
the voyage complete
with the audacious assumption
that I know what's ahead
please spare me
the spoiled ending
until I am dead.

Instead,
why not set your sails
to your true north?
Hope & lean into the gales
that ingnite your soul's hearth,

and if the sea derails
you can always adjust,
charting in your rutter
a unwavering trust
that life works
in allegiance
to your favor

and please,
choose to be braver
than the little voice
in your mind
anxiously awaiting
the destination
before it is time;

you sit & watch
maps & clocks
missing out
on the sublime.

Remember,
this is the great voyage
of your life!
This is your only ship.
You are your only captain.
This is your only trip.
(Trust me, it helps
to loosen your grip).

Maybe you don't need
to have it all figured out.
Maybe you don't want to know
what happens next.

Maybe you just need
to be here now
paying heed
to this present dream;
trusting your compass,
setting your sails
& letting fate
take care of the details.

The Fisherman

What if life
is simpler than you think?

Let go & you'll rise
add weight & you'll sink.

You find what you look for
and the rest you ignore.

What you attract depends
on your bait & your lure.

And how often are you
out by the shore?

Throwing cast after cast
into the sea's mighty roar?

Your hopes & dreams
will not be delivered to your door.

You must get up to try & try
and know what you are striving for.

A Wild Cloak

All desire to be seen
swallowed by the ecstasy
of a wild cloak

(Can I hide behind
the wisteria vines
forever?)

Let them
entangle
my curls

Let them
clamber
inside of me

Overgrow
my thoughts
with blossoms

Fill my skull
with sweet musk

They leave
no space
for worry

no space
for aches

(Don't look at me!)
I have become
a flower
again:

fragile, intricate, ethereal
fading quickly in a vase

When I Die

I'm not too concerned about
what happens when I die
(why do humans seek
immortal life?)

as long as my body
is not locked away inside
some coffin
where the earth cannot reach me

wouldn't it be much more peaceful
to just rot?
cradled in a microbial cot
I will become soil—never again distraught
by the worries & woes
of human's fickle thoughts

When I die
plant my body bare
under a redwood tree
let the mushrooms eat me
I am not concerned
with legalities
(my body will be gone
and my soul free)
so carve a poem in stone
and just let me be

I've got a new challenge
Since everyone loves to compete
Tell me, how long could you sit still
Under a tree?

One minute? Five?
Would you begin reaching for your phone?
Ten minutes? Twenty?
With your thoughts all alone

Surely after thirty minutes
You could feel the tree breathe
And after forty five,
99% of people would leave
Searching for a distraction
The next dopamine fix
Checking their watch
(the point was never to time it)

Only when time ceases to exist
Can you really win the game
When you've noticed the miracle
In every leaf vein—Don't you see?
We've been distracted our whole lives

Quiet peace is what we need
Productivity is
Sitting still under a tree
Remembering how
To just
Be.

Expansion does not happen over night or even over years. It happens through questions, and a willingness to abandon everything you thought you knew;

to humbly admit that there may not be an ultimate truth. Rather, the truth is in each person's journey—the way they sort through and make peace with the hundred trillion things.

You say you're an adventurer...

The world is so wide that you could **travel it for the rest of your life** and *still never know* its every shoreline, village, forest, crevice, peak; the **spectacular secrets stashed in hidden pockets** where no man goes or *even seeks.*

Equally, **my soul is so deep,** you could dive in its oceans *for the rest of eternity* and still never grasp my fervor for living, **the expanse of my heart**, my intricate mind, my inner gardens of art.

You say you're an adventurer, **but will you ever take the trip?**

(*Will you even take the trip?*)

I am the type to weep softly at dusk
when the sky turns crimson and pink

as my favorite star descends
down, down in the horizon he sinks

our marble-like world
spins around him
we twirl! in ecstasy

you look at me
salty drops in my eyes
of course, the tears
I try to hide

you ask me "why?"
"are you alright?"
your deep voice makes me weak
golden hour shimmers on your cheeks

I shouldn't be
ashamed to cry
it's just that I—
I fall in love every time

the sunset never gets old
but the wind now is growing cold

and where your skin
once touched mine
is now only bathed in moonlight

tomorrow I'll weep with joy
at the sunrise
hoping somewhere

maybe
you're watching it, too

Love Me Like the Moon

most of us are meteors
barreling or meandering
through time & space, randomly
colliding in temporary
supernova blasts, brief
passion & stardust
(does anything last?)

they say Moon met Earth millenia ago,
kissed once, burst apart
yet fell effortlessly in flow
though the cosmos of a trillion forces
tried to pull them apart
their loyalty never leaves orbit
they're *that* sure of it!
(can love be written in the stars?)

they say the Moon
has no light of her own
absorbing & reflecting Sun's rays
she magnifies & multiplies, never takes away
she must be a woman, a goddess, a lover
every night a new phase
in her monthly dance around the globe
she's followed me faithfully all my days
(love like that is just a fantasy, I've been told)

but I dream anyways
she'll fill up my cup with lunar light rays
I don't want a mere taste

even after all those years lost in the dark
she still lights my way
understanding my waves
of gasping tides;
wolf songs she orchestrates

her molten core like the Earth, holding
all my dreams half baked
in the ovens of destiny
(let moonlight take the rest of me)

in this world of halftones,
supernova blasts
who will love me like the Moon?
(I want something that lasts)

Defiantly walk away
from the comfortable paved road.
Choose a way of life that aligns
with the fire in your soul.

There is no peace or individuality
on a crowded straight interstate.
Wouldn't you rather take a back road,
ditch the car, hop a freight?

Take a meandering footpath
to a billowing willow grove
beckoning you to sit down,
(finally) refuge from the droves

of a billion lost sheep
blindly following the herd
in the quiet beneath the trees
Nature's answers emerge.

The highway makes it seem
like there is only one road
yet the footpaths reveal
there are a million ways to go.

An unassuming morning hum
prisms of an old record
coaxed by needle into song:

"Mother, should I trust the government?"

A crow
smashed into my window,
fell to the ground stiff & lifeless.

Mother Earth said,
"No."

When normalcy drowns in shallow waters,
the wild & strange ones will inhert in the Earth.

Always leave people & places
better than you found them, even
if they don't do the same for you.

The trails of seeds scattered
from your calloused hands are destined
to sprout from rubble; burst through.

Though you may never see the tree,
nor harvest the fruits, you will
always know in your heart
that you nourished the roots.

How We Change the World

Hulls

Hulls of ships or
hulls of seeds
holding something
that needs protection

(should the shell
around my heart
be thicker?)
                              and me?
                              I am whole
Conifers are called   but hull-less
gymnosperms
because their seeds   the only cage
are naked   around my heart
inside the cones   is rib bones

(their strategy   I am a naked seed
seems to work—   ancient drifting
they began   in the wind
millenia ago)   searching for soil
                              to call home
but all the newer plants
encase their seeds
in the guards of fruit

(the modern way
is safer, they say
now the hulled seeds rule)

Spice

Mediocrity does not interest me
I grow weary of stale repetition

I am willing to dive headfirst
into the unknown abyss
just to escape the vacuous condition.

Why does the world settle
for the shallow surface,
denying their inner truth?

Halftone love & droning talk
tastes bland

I want depth,

spice,

realness

without excuse.

As you get closer to the path
you are meant to walk,
you will naturally feel lighter.

Layers & layers of false personas shed.
Pounds & pounds of baggage dropped.
All the fistfuls of fears & opinions
& confusion & questioning
will finally fall
from the grip of your hands;
your arms sway freely now.

The weight of all the things
that weren't right for you,
finally lifted
from your bones.

The itchy costumes
& uncomfortable masks
& useless maps
to undesirable destinations—
they all decay
in the dirt
behind you.

They are not yours;
they never were.

All that is meant for you
will rest lightly
on your skin
& fit perfectly
in your hands.
It will not
weigh you down.

You will know when
you rediscover your purpose,
because it will feel
effortless,
like breathing.

Because of the Mud

I promise, one day you'll wake up & the sun
will be bursting in & you'll be so glad
that life dragged you through the mud

because walking is easy now;
your legs are strong.

You became who you are meant to be,
not in spite of your struggle
but because of it.

Nothing is forever,
perhaps a miracle on its own.

If the mountains were perennially
smothered in meadows,
would we still rush to their peaks
for summer's fleeting burst?

If the sky was perpetually
smeared in rainbows,
would dusk & dawn cease
to captivate us?

If life on Earth was eternal,
there would be no impetus
to make anything of Now

(because there would
always be more time)

But nothing is forever
because the ephemeral conditions
of our humble existence
are precisely
what make it all so precious.

I like my feet dirty
it means I walk with the Earth.

I like my hair curly
tangled & salty in the surf.

I'd rather swim in the river
over some chlorinated pool.

Society leaves me empty.
Only Nature keeps me full.

Sensual Intricacy

come lay with me
in the grass for awhile
I'll show you a whole world
of magic & desire:

do you see how
dandelion anthers
stand erect
with their yellow pollen
wind dancers above
cushions of a thousand ovules
waiting to be loved?

(but you must be hushed
to hear her petals unfurling;
she won't let
just anybody
in)

now notice
when the floral stem
is snapped
it exudes a milky creamy sap

& nearby each bug climbs
each blade of stiff grass
a big one & a small one,
a tiny one, too
like a stack of Russian dolls
(all the layers inside of you)

& look out there—somewhere
in the thickets of green
calling for her lover,
a cardinal sings;
a bear births her clumsy cubs
in the safety of spring

& everything is breathing, alive
butterflies drinking
nectar, blossoms
dreaming
delicate
sensual intricacy
yearning for pollination,
that intimacy

(plus there is you & there is me
this exquisite
unnameable desire
flowing between)

Saturate me in rainbows of sunrise
Soak my heart in the glow of moonlight

Fill my ears with whispering leaf songs
Quench my thirst with sips of the sea's calm

I will lay in the sand and release all
Like the Earth's soft truth, I will be raw

Look at you!

You shed all your old skins,
dropped patterns & leaves.

You stood through the winter,
frigid & bare,
you thawed with the spring.

You dug deep in the soil
and plucked every last weed.

You amended your heart
with compost & dream seeds.

Now look at you!

At last,

You're Blooming!
You're Blooming!

How do you make peace
with the madness
of the world?

I rush down
to the river
every afternoon
to feel the mud
between my toes
remembering soon

I'll be just another
particle of silt
drifting in the currents
of eternity.

Who is the beholder of beauty
without eyes in human form?

In the mirrorless woods
I love who I am
without looking;

I forget my face
as I admire
the graceful bow
of a drooping hemlock branch
wet with sparkling raindrops

I ask her:
isn't everyone beautiful
in their own right?

Do you have space for newness? Or is your world too cluttered with the past? **Let the dream burn a great big hole of light within you.** Let it remain vacant, shining, a beaming welcome lamp from the porch of your heart (easy to spot in this gnarled world of dark).

Emptiness holds no negatives. **It is the cosmic question mark.** Meadows bloom in the clearings where there is more light (there must be room for new gifts to germinate).

I once jumped from a boulder
into the sea

Forests of kelp cradled me
in slimy silky bliss

A frenzy of salty green
sinuous & supple

They swaddled
my lithe limbs
in the sweetest embrace

Floating free in the ocean
intermingling our fates

Solace

I love the night but
morning is my solace

Many stay up late
but few emerge early
except, of course
all the wild things
who wake without names
or addresses

Can you imagine the bliss
of a leaf
when the first sunbeam
caresses her skin
after a long night
with chloroplasts asleep
stomata huddled from the breeze
(morning like a great sigh of relief)

Can you imagine the shock
of a shrub
in his first winter
when everything turns solid with ice
for him, spring is morning
his thaw like a caffeine spike
(every day and night thereafter
just a blinking of the sky)

Can you imagine the longing
of a river
galloping infinitely toward the sea
the way she craves
to meet salty waves
gushing with relief
when finally she kisses the ocean
at the mouth of some quiet sunrise beach

Can you imagine the moon or the sun
elusive in their embrace
circling & circling
night & day
like forbidden lovers at play
(is that why they
paint such a display
at dusk & dawn?)

Yes, I love the night but
morning is my solace

When I wake early under the trees
the earth has so much peace
she doesn't even need to sleep

Leaves keep glowing
shrubs keep growing
rivers keep flowing
and how lucky am I?
to keep going

To wake again to a new day's hum
that always seems to come

Solace, I cannot bare to miss

Choose the Marvelous

Ordinary life does not interest me.

I want passion & challenge & grit
I want strangeness & wonder & adventure

There is no time for mundanity
I am seeking the magnificent
Romance & poetry
The magic of existence

I cannot wade in shallow pools
I cannot hope for far off someday
We mistakenly think we have infinite time
But I will not wait until one day

I do not want the ordinary
I choose the marvelous!

I will not die wishing I had followed the rules.

Sometimes we need nothing more
than the sun on our faces
breeze at our backs
to remember who we are
and where we've been

The road unfolds in ways
I never could've imagined then
but I follow faithfully
the unexpected curves
and spontaneous whims

The Sun Will Always Rise Again

Now Everything Makes Sense

Now I am the fern frond unfurling
My soul's work like breathing
Inhale emotions, exhale words
There is no more wheezing.

Now the days brighten intensely
Night's darkness like blinking
Past like glass, future like quartz
Fate's surprises winking.

Now love buzzes infinitely within
My heart like a garden flourishing
Souls the flowers, I am the bee
Our symbiosis deeply nourishing.

Now everything makes sense
My mind a tranquil knowing
No more agony or confusion
My heart's forests regrowing.

The Grizzly Queen

came to visit me
on the eve of Gemini's return.
The image of her colossal form
forever in my memory burned.

She walked without hurry,
browsed without haste.
Satisfied by the flowers,
my blood she did not taste.

But very close, she came
in dusk's fading light.
The river sparkled sapphire,
her claws, ivory white.

Ruler of the Rockies,
Queen of the Spruce,
nose to the ground,
persistent in her route.

In her den, she nearly dies
yet reemerges every spring,
she savagely protects her cubs,
her territory & her dreams.

Yes, the Grizzly Queen
walks alone in her power;
the moose flee the woods
and the black bears cower.

She knows who she is,
the wild glows from her fur;
unbothered by attention,
she is Naturally Her.

Never be ashamed of
where you've been;
this version of you
could not prosper
without the
decayed leaves
of who you used to be.

Inside you lives every person you once were:

> One year old You like a **blank canvas**,
> Five year old You *exploring* the world,
> Ten year old You who **knew almost nothing**,
> Teenager You who **thought** you *knew it all*,
> Twenty year old You **completely lost**,
> Thirty year old You *finding peace*,
> All the Yous growing **older & wiser** with time.

Every past version of you has **decomposed at your feet** and nourished the person *you were always meant to be*. Yet so many people are embarrassed of who they've been, trying to erase the past, burying it beneath **layers and layers** of shame, forgetting to recognize that the **lessons we learned from our mistakes** made us who we are today. Remember,

Trees need mulch

They Tried

When they tried to pot me up
My roots burst through the cracks
When they tried to cut me down
My bark broke their axe

When they tried to imitate my route
The sand concealed my tracks
They tried to make me match their stride
But I refused to follow the pack

Definition, I elude
Uniqueness, I exude
My vivid glow cannot be subdued

I wear no disguise,
Yet my joy, they despise
My truth I do not compromise

I play with form,
I break the norm,
I am at once, calm & storm

Yet they still tried to bury me
Forgetting the soil was my home
Then they sprayed me with poison
Yet my sprouts grew from the loam

& when they tried to burn me to the ground
The ash enriched my roots
I regrew
I bloomed

And just like Maya Angelou: Still I rise!
Though many tears I cried
They were only water
For this vivacious soul of mine

Be defiant in your gladness!
Dandelions bloom from ditches, dammit
I'll dance at the world's end.

Just like the Dandelion
rises obstinately
from roadside rubble
glowing glorious gold
amidst grey—
I *choose* to see the good.

They say the world is ending
maybe tomorrow, maybe today?
Humans lost in absurd evils
wars & hate, everyone they betray
(even the flowers they spray—
all for what?)

Well, I don't know.
I turned off the news long ago.

I know they thought
they could smother our light.
Ha! I say the good is still winning.

There is still innocent
sacredness swimming
in a child's smile
who wishes on feathery
seedheads
brimming
with 20,000 dreams
to billow in the breeze
flying like birds bound
for better days.

But today is just as good as any, ain't it?
You're reading this, aren't ya?
You're breathing, I assume?
Even my battered heart still beats stubbornly
behind my ribcage (and apparently yours does, too.)

The world is cruel, yes
but the Optimist can be crueler.
She'll spread smiling seeds like wildfire;
sprout her children in vibrant armies
growing rampant,
bursting higher
than grasses on sterile lawns
pathetic pavement
makes her yawn;
Her taproot is unrelenting.
She'll refill the world
with color.

There is suffering, yes.
Do not turn a blind eye.
But can we talk
about the good?

Medicine still grows
obstinately at our feet.
Dandelions still flourish
from concrete.

Maybe it's all doomed
or maybe it's not.
But for once,
can we just talk
about the good?

01. Life has **more beautiful things** in store for you than you can possibly imagine. **Stay true to this season**, and trust the timing of your evolution.
02. We are all made of the **same things**; in different quantities and proportions.
03. Your path was **made only for you**. Nobody else knows how to walk it.
04. **Wounds are portals**. If you want to live a deep, expansive, profound existence, you must be willing to explore the depths of self.
05. Wildfires are a natural part of the ecological cycles of **renewal** and **regrowth**. Let go of what no longer suits you, and let it nourish your next phase.
06. You **do not need** the validation of any human. Your existence on Earth is enough proof that **Nature needs you**. You are welcome here.
07. Do not strive to impress anyone (except the **trees** and **wildflowers**; their opinion matters).
08. Softness is **not weakness**. Water flows gently over stone, yet it has the power to shape the whole Earth.
09. The **seed** does not know the magnificence of what it will become. It looks completely different than the flower or the fruit. **Be patient with your unfurling**. Allow yourself the freedom to change.
10. **Play**. Retain your **childlike wonder** for the world.
11. When society drains you, run back to the wild to be refilled. **Protect the Earth**, and it will protect you.
12. Do not let anyone make you feel small. The microscopic fungal spore is **just as important** as the gigantic grey whale. We are all part of the ecological web. No single being is more valuable than another.

Of course, the Earth loves you back!

How else could you explain the offerings of floral fragrance, misty mountains, steaming springs, and decadent berries?

You are allowed to feel joy, pleasure, bliss!

What else could the fish & birds be doing when we aren't looking?

The grasses are dancing in the breeze
and we should be, too.

Paradise is a State of Mind

Paradise is a state of mind
Not where you go or what you find
The oasis you must create inside
With conscious effort, you can decide:

I will be free and shine my light
Behind a mask, I refuse to hide
Though life may bring lessons and strife
They can make you bitter or make you wise

Perception is only in your eyes
Perhaps the magic is in surprise
So how will you play
this game called life?

Paradise is a state of mind
Let your bliss be your guide
Let your inner child shine
Because one day we all must die

Tell me,
are you just living
or are you fully alive?

Logan Hailey is an author, poet, naturalist, and vivacious vagabond. She travels in her self-built van from the farthest wildernesses to the coziest towns, seeking soulful connection to the Earth and its wild inhabitants.

An exuberant adventurer, forager, botanist, and organic farmer, she harvests inspiration from Mother Nature's gentle, grounding flow. Most days you will find her bare foot with pen and paper by a river, forest, or sea with her furry yin & yang sidekicks, Bluegrass & Banjo.

This is Logan's first book, motivated by her gratitude for the natural world that healed her aching soul and rekindled her zest for life.

Keep up with the adventure **@naturallylogan** on social media and **www.naturallylogan.com**

Stay Wild & Vivacious!
xoxo Logan Hailey

Credits

Cover Illustration by Erick Solar
Commissioned with Full Permission and Licensing Rights

Photographs on pages 51, 78, 79, 107, 123, 124 & 126
by Mark Collins (@wild.life.mark), Used with Full Permission and Licensing Rights

Butterfly and galaxy artwork on pages 26, 27, 80 & 81
by Britt West (@plantposseart)
Used with Full Permission and Licensing Rights

Botanical linework drawings on pages 2 & 121
by Eileen Schaeffer Brantley (@herbgirleileen)
Used with Full Permission and Licensing Rights

Cyanotype artwork on pages 25, 41, 95 & 111
by Sarah Padilla (@sarahpadilla.creates)
Used with Full Permission and Licensing Rights

Photographs on pages 18, 63, 66, 130 & 131
Courtesy of Shutterstock
Used with Full Permission and Licensing Rights

Photographs on pages 5, 6, 9, 15, 16, 21, 29, 30, 32, 34, 35, 39, 40, 43, 46, 47, 49, 53, 55, 57, 58, 65, 68, 69, 71, 72, 73, 74, 76, 77, 82, 85, 87, 88, 91, 93, 96, 99, 103, 104, 108, 112, 113, 117, 118, 129, 132, 134, 137, 139 by the author
Copyright © 2024 Logan Hailey